bubblefacts...

# HUMAN BODY

PUBLISHING

First published in 2004 by
Miles Kelly Publishing Ltd
Bardfield Centre, Great Bardfield, Essex, CM7 4SL

Copyright © Miles Kelly Publishing Ltd 2004

2 4 6 8 10 9 7 5 3 1

Editorial Director:
Anne Marshall

Senior Editor:
Belinda Gallagher

Editorial Assistant:
Lisa Clayden

Designer:
Debbie Meekcoms

Cartoons:
Mike Davis

Production:
Estela Godoy

ISBN 1-84236-392-1

Printed in China

British Library Cataloguing-in-Publication Data
A catalogue record for this book is available from the British Library

Indexer: Jane Parker

www.mileskelly.net
info@mileskelly.net

# Contents

# Covered from head...
## ...to toe!

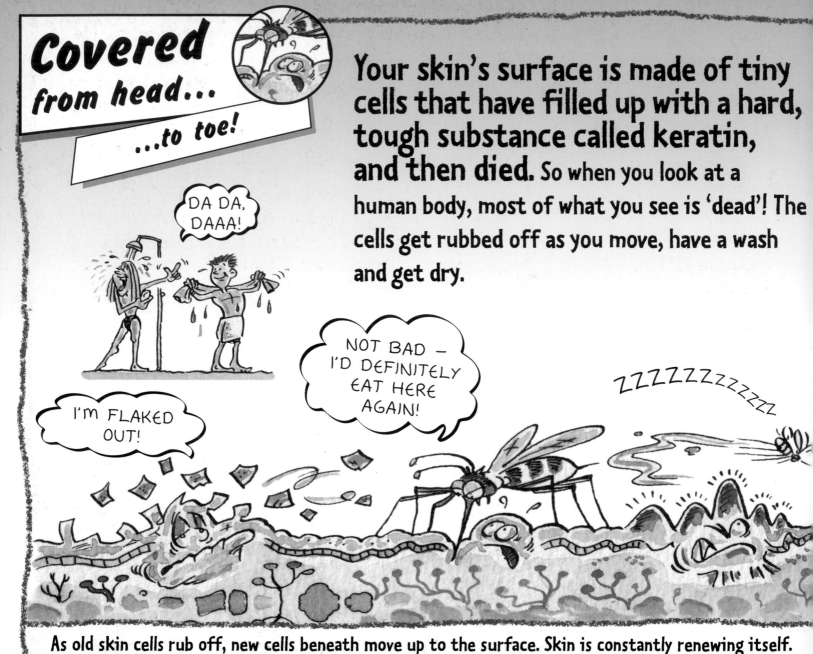

Your skin's surface is made of tiny cells that have filled up with a hard, tough substance called keratin, **and then died.** So when you look at a human body, most of what you see is 'dead'! The cells get rubbed off as you move, have a wash and get dry.

As old skin cells rub off, new cells beneath move up to the surface. Skin is constantly renewing itself.

Skin helps to keep our bodies the same temperature. If we become too hot, sweat oozes onto the skin and, as it dries, it draws heat from the body. Our skin is also covered in fine hair. When we are cold, these hairs stand on end, trapping heat and holding it to the skin where it is warmed by blood vessels close to the surface.

Skin gives us our sense of touch. Millions of microscopic sensors in the lower layer of skin – the dermis – are joined by nerves to the brain. Different sensors detect different kinds of touch – from a light stroke to heavy pressure. Pain sensors detect when skin is damaged, such as through a burn.

BANG! BANG!

REALLY! SO INCONSIDERATE. THE NOISE!

AAAGH! CAREFUL!

Skin keeps delicate body parts from being damaged. Pain sensors detect when skin is hurt.

# Hard as nails

**There are about 120,000 hairs on your head!** You also have eyebrow hairs and eyelash hairs. And everyone, even a baby, has tiny hairs all over their bodies – 20 million of them!

## Can you believe it?

A scalp hair grows for up to five years before it falls out. Left uncut it would be one metre in length.

WICKED STYLE!

COOL! WISH I COULD SAY THE SAME ABOUT YOURS.

I THINK YOU HAVE MY SHARE TOO...

Hair can be curly, straight or wavy. It can be red, black, fair or brown. Some people have no hair!

Men can grow beards and moustaches on their faces. Some women spend hours styling their hair!

Hair grows all the time - and so do nails. Your nails grow half a millimetre a week - faster in summer!

# Bony framework

## skeleton facts

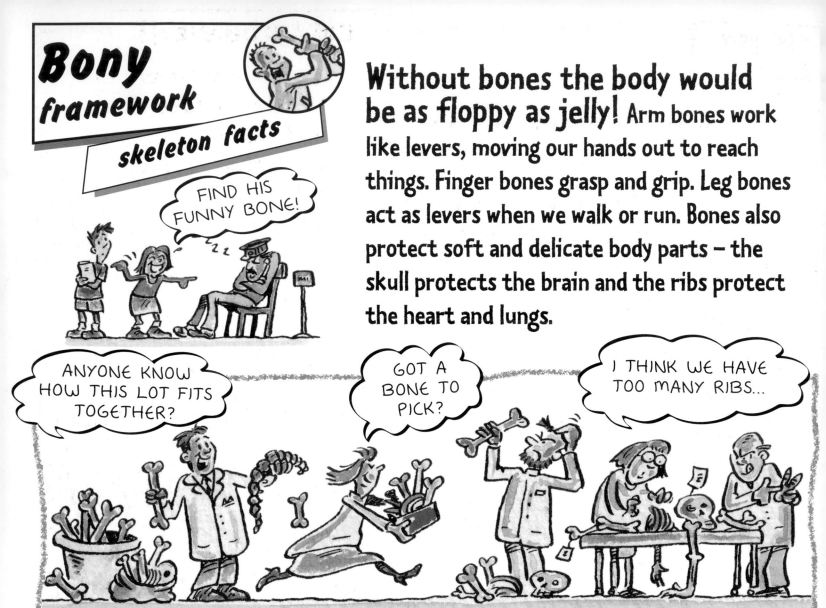

**Without bones the body would be as floppy as jelly!** Arm bones work like levers, moving our hands out to reach things. Finger bones grasp and grip. Leg bones act as levers when we walk or run. Bones also protect soft and delicate body parts – the skull protects the brain and the ribs protect the heart and lungs.

All the bones together in our bodies make up the skeleton. There are 206 bones in total.

Bone has a hard outside layer, a spongy layer beneath this, and a soft jelly-like middle section. Some bones make blood cells in this soft centre. Doctors can also take pictures of our bones, called X-rays. These show if a bone is broken or damaged.

Babies have 350 bones when they are born. As they grow, the bones fuse (join) together until there are 206 adult bones.

Bone is very strong and light. In fact one kilogram of bone is stronger than one kilogram of concrete!

# Bendy body

## joint action!

**Without joints you wouldn't be able to move.** Joints between bones allow the skeleton to bend – and you have more than 150 joints in your body. The largest are in the hips and knees. The smallest are in the fingers, toes – and between the tiny bones in your ear that help you to hear.

There are different kinds of joints. A ball-and-socket joint in the shoulder lets the arm move in circles.

The brain controls all our muscles and joints. It sends instructions to them, telling us how to move our bodies.

The bones in a joint are held together by stretchy strips called ligaments. These let the bones move, but stop them moving too far apart. Some joints, such as in the knee, have bony coverings called cartilage. These help the knee to lock straight so that we can stand up straight without too much effort.

SWISH! SWISH!

FLYING TUTUS!

I SAID HIGHER!

KEEP YOUR HAIR ON!

A hinge joint lets the knee move backwards and forwards – but not sideways.

# Muscle power

## flex those pecs

Can you believe it?

You use almost all the muscles in your face to frown, but only half of them to grin!

Almost half the body's weight is muscles, and there are more than 640 of them! Muscles have one important job, which is to get shorter, or contract. A muscle cannot get longer. It's this contracting action that powers everything we do, from running to blinking.

CHEAT.

SO WHAT!

THUMP!!

Muscles contract, pulling on bones to move them. As this happens, the muscle bulges in the middle.

Exercise makes muscles strong. A weightlifter can lift three times his own weight over his head.

The pecs (pectoralis major) are in the chest. The biceps (biceps brachii) are in the top of your arm.

# Breath of fresh air
## breathe in...out!

The body cannot survive more than a minute or two without breathing. We breathe to take air into our bodies. The main parts of the respiratory (breathing) system are the two lungs in the chest. Each one is shaped like a cone, with the pointed end at shoulder level.

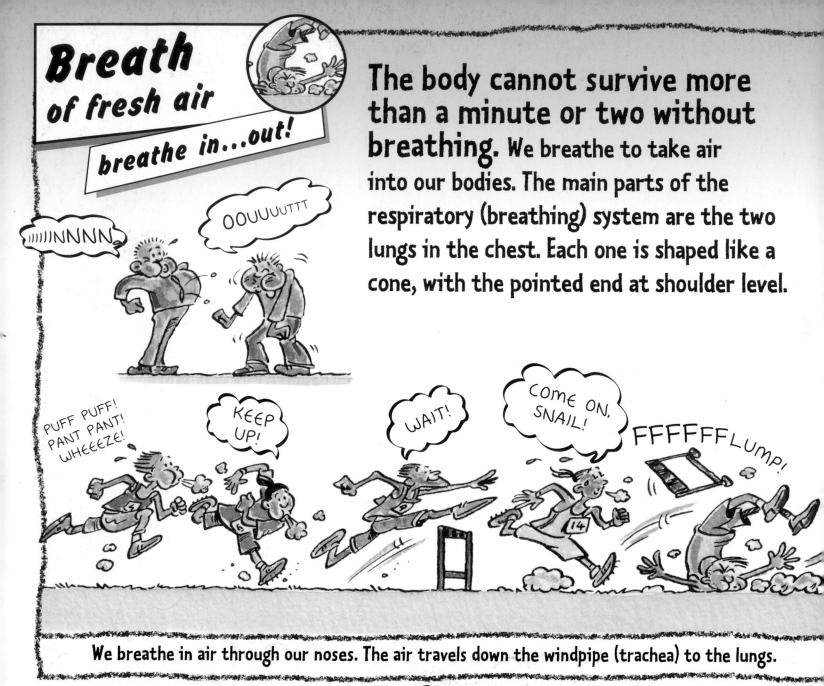

We breathe in air through our noses. The air travels down the windpipe (trachea) to the lungs.

Air breathed in and out through the night by a sleeping person fills an average-sized room. This is why some people sleep with the window open!

The more active you are, the more oxygen your body needs. You breathe in more to replace oxygen used by the muscles for energy. As you rest or sleep, each breath sends about half a litre of air in and out, 15 to 20 times a minute. After great activity you might take in three litres or more of air, 50 times or more a minute!

MOVE IT, LOSER!

AAAGH!

CHEAT!

YES! YES! YES!

PUFF! HUFF!

After great activity, such as running, you need more oxygen. You take in deeper breaths, faster.

# Food glorious food
## yum yum!

All machines need fuel to make them work. The body is like a living machine whose fuel is food. Food gives us energy for body processes and for breathing, moving, talking and every other action we make. Food also provides raw materials that the body uses to maintain itself, grow and repair daily wear-and-tear.

A healthy diet needs a variety of foods – after all, we wouldn't put the wrong type of fuel into a car!

There are six groups of nutrients (goodness) in food that the body needs: carbohydrates, such as sugars and starches, to give us energy; proteins for growth and repair; small amounts of certain fats; vitamins to fight germs and disease; minerals for healthy bones and teeth; fibre for good digestion.

The human body never grows as fast again as it does during the first weeks in the womb. If it carried on, you would be as big as a mountain!

EAT MORE FRUIT AND VEG!

SHOCK! HORROR!

A HEALTHY DIET MEANS A HEALTHY HEART...

IT MUST BE MY COOKING!

Eating too much food may make the body overweight. This could lead to illnesses such as heart disease.

# Bite, chew, gulp!

## what a mouthful!

MUNCH! CRUNCH!

GUZZLE! GLUG!

**The hardest parts of your body are the ones that make holes in your food – teeth.** They have a covering of whitish enamel, which is stronger than most kinds of rocks! Teeth need to last a lifetime of biting, nibbling, gnashing, munching and chewing.

CLEAN TOOTH!

ROTTEN TOOTH

AAGH!

BABY TOOTH

LONG IN THE TOOTH

A tooth is very much alive. Inside is a supply of blood and nerves that feel heat, cold – and pain.

There are four main shapes of teeth. The front ones are incisors and each has a straight, sharp edge to cut through food. Next are the canines (see right). These are tall and pointed and are used for tearing and pulling food. Behind them are premolars and molars, which grind and crush food.

Teeth are very strong and should last a lifetime. But they need to be cleaned properly and regularly. Germs called bacteria live on old bits of food in the mouth. These make a waste product that is like an acid, which eats into the enamel. Brushing teeth twice a day helps prevent this – and stops you getting toothache!

SHINY TOOTH

SHARP TOOTH!

STRONG TOOTH

SENSITIVE TOOTH

CROWN-ED TOOTH!

At about seven years old, baby teeth begin to fall out and are replaced by a set of 32 adult teeth.

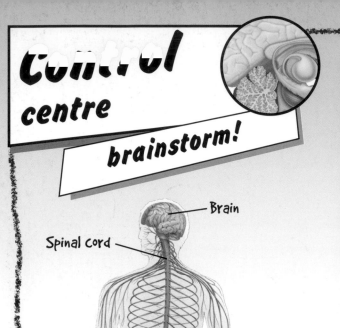

Brain

Spinal cord

Nerves

**Your brain is as big as your two fists side by side.** It helps you think, learn, remember, feel emotions, have ideas, sleep and dream. Yet the brain looks like a wrinkly lump of grey-pink jelly! Its amazing nerve activity uses up one-fifth of all the energy needed by the body.

The brain is protected by the skull, a thick case of bone. The skull is divided into 28 bones – but it is those at the top, called the cranium, which protect the brain from damage.

Nerves send high-speed messages to the brain along a network called the nervous system. This system controls everything we do – from blinking to running. The whole system is made up of the brain, the spinal cord and the nerves.

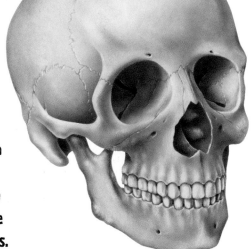

Your brain is inside your head and is protected from damage by the thick bones of your skull.

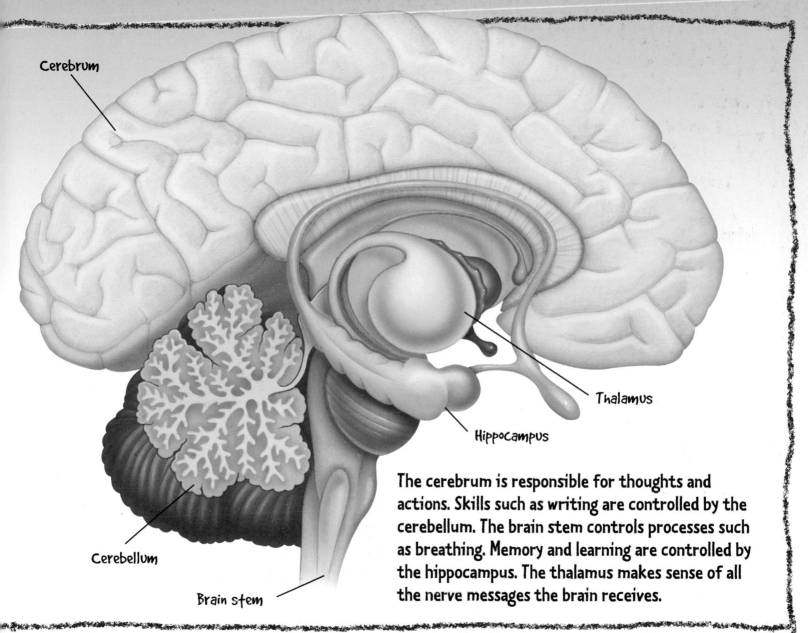

Cerebrum

Thalamus

Hippocampus

Cerebellum

Brain stem

The cerebrum is responsible for thoughts and actions. Skills such as writing are controlled by the cerebellum. The brain stem controls processes such as breathing. Memory and learning are controlled by the hippocampus. The thalamus makes sense of all the nerve messages the brain receives.

Every second, your brain receives, sorts and sends millions of nerve signals. It controls everything you do.

# Rumbling tummy

## the food chain

**The digestive system is like a 9-metre-long tunnel through the body.** It includes parts of the body that bite food, chew it, swallow it, churn it up and break it down with natural juices and acids, take in its goodness, and then get rid of the leftovers.

A LIGHT SNACK!

YUM YUM! CRUNCH! MUNCH!

APPLE... AGAIN.

HI HO HI HO...

In the stomach, food is broken down into a thick liquid. This liquid is passed to the small intestine.

The stomach produces gastric juices. These include an acid that breaks down food and kills any harmful germs that may cause infection. Muscular walls in the stomach work with the gastric juices to churn food into a thick liquid, ready to go to the small intestine.

The lining of the small intestine is covered in tiny finger-like structures called villi. They take the goodness from the liquid food and carry it into the bloodstream, where it is used by the body. The leftovers, or waste, now enter the large intestine. Here, water and salt are absorbed until the waste becomes solid, ready to leave the body the next time you go to the toilet.

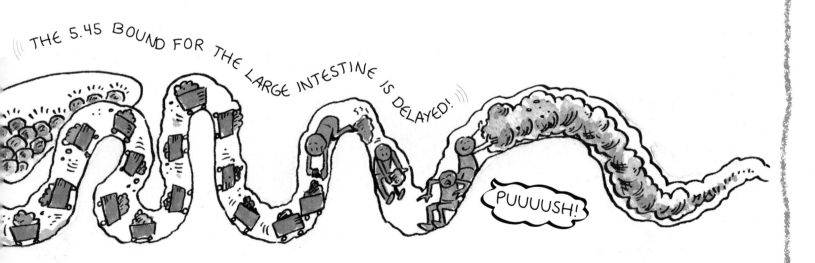

The small intestine absorbs the food's goodness and pushes the leftovers to the large intestine.

# Blood, beautiful... ...blood!

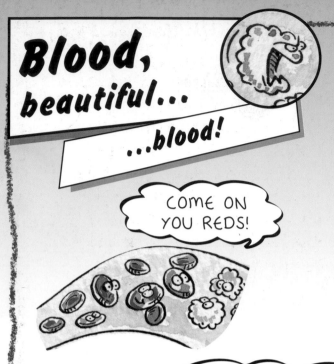

The heart beats to pump blood all around the body and pass its vital oxygen and nutrients to every part. The same blood goes round and round, or circulates, in its network of blood vessels. So the heart, blood vessels and blood are known as the circulatory system.

Blood has three main parts – red cells, white cells to fight germs, and platelets that help blood to clot.

Blood travels from the heart through strong, thick-walled vessels called arteries. These divide again and again, becoming smaller and smaller until they form tiny vessels, narrower than hairs, called capillaries. Oxygen and goodness from food seep through the thin walls of the capillaries into the body parts around them.

Blood is cleaned by the kidneys, two organs in the middle of the body, towards your back. They filter the blood and make a liquid called urine that contains waste substances and spare water. Urine trickles from the kidneys into a stretchy bag called the bladder. It's stored here until you go to the toilet.

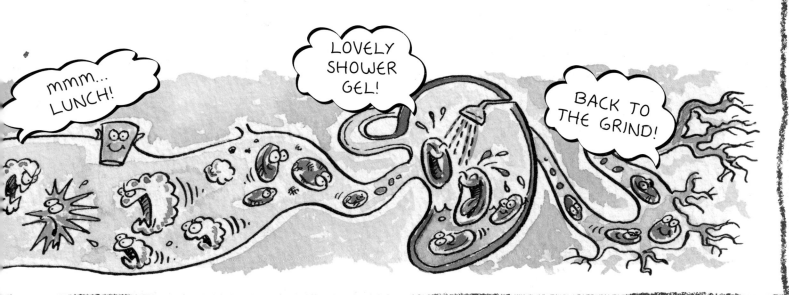

As well as delivering oxygen and food, blood spreads heat evenly around the body.

# Heart
## of the matter
### your beating body

**Your heart is as big as your fist.** It's a hollow bag of strong muscle, called cardiac muscle. This muscle contracts once every second or more, all through life. The contraction, or heartbeat, squeezes blood inside the heart out into the arteries. As the heart relaxes it fills again with blood from the veins.

Cardiac (heart) muscle never tires – the heart is constantly pumping blood around the body.

When the body is active and needs more oxygen, the heart beats faster to supply the muscles.

Your heart needs the right food for energy – and even at rest it is busy, although it beats more slowly.

# Looking and listening

*hear hear!*

STOP WHINGING!

The body finds out about the world around it by using its senses – the main sense is eyesight. The eyes detect brightness, colours and patterns of light. These are then changed into nerve signals that travel to the brain. In fact more of the brain is dedicated to vision than any other sense.

When light enters the eye, the optic nerve sends messages to the brain, which are sorted into images.

Sound waves enter the ear through flaps on the side of the head. The waves travel along the ear canal to the eardrum, which vibrates, passing messages onto three tiny bones, the smallest in the body. These then pass vibrations to the cochlea, a curly, fluid-filled area. The vibrations pass through the fluid to tiny hairs cells that make signals, which flash along the auditory nerve to the brain.

More than half of the knowledge, information and memories stored in the brain enters the body through the eyes.

WWWWWWEEEEEEEE

WOOF!

HIS BARK IS WORSE THAN HIS BITE!

The loudness of sound is measured in decibels (dB). A whisper is 20 dB and a jet engine is 130 dB!

# Smell and taste

**You cannot see smells, particles floating in the air, but your nose can smell them.** Your nose can detect more than 10,000 different scents. Smell can warn us if food is bad and perhaps dangerous to eat. That's why we sniff a new food, almost without thinking, before trying it.

YOU'RE SOOO GENEROUS!

DISGUSTING!

DELICIOUS!

Smell particles land on areas called receptors, in the nose. Nerves then carry messages to the brain.

Taste buds coat the tongue. These are covered in hair cells that send flavour messages to the brain.

The tongue detects sweet, salty, bitter and sour flavours. It also recognises texture and temperature.

# Index